SATURN AND ITS RINGS

ASTRONOMY FOR KIDS BOOKS GRADE 4
CHILDREN'S ASTRONOMY & SPACE BOOKS

BABY PROFESSOR

First Edition, 2019

Published in the United States by Speedy Publishing LLC, 40 E Main Street, Newark, Delaware 19711 USA.

© 2019 Baby Professor Books, an imprint of Speedy Publishing LLC

Baby Professor Books are available at special discounts when purchased in bulk for industrial and sales-promotional use. For details contact our Special Sales Team at Speedy Publishing LLC, 40 E Main Street, Newark, Delaware 19711 USA. Telephone (888) 248-4521 Fax: (210) 519-4043. www.speedybookstore.com

10 9 8 7 6 * 5 4 3 2 1

Print Edition: 9781541953314
Digital Edition: 9781541956315

See the world in pictures. Build your knowledge in style.
https://www.speedypublishing.com/

TABLE OF CONTENTS

The Basics About Saturn.............................6

Saturn's Orbit...................................10

A Gassy Giant...................................14

A Lightweight Planet.............................17

The Discovery of Saturn..........................21

Discovering Saturn's Rings.......................25

What Are Saturn's Rings?.........................30

The Moons of Saturn.............................36

Discovering Titan...............................41

Saturn's Titan..................................44

Naming Saturn..................................48

Saturn's Rings and Moons........................51

Travel to Saturn................................54

Summary......................................63

Of all eight planets in our solar system, the Milky Way, Saturn is the most recognizable because it has the biggest, flashiest, most unusual accessories—rings! The rings of Saturn are just one of the reasons why this large and impressive planet is so remarkable. Let's learn all about Saturn—its position in the night sky, what it's made of, how it was discovered, and all about those rings.

Saturn in the space abstract art.
Elements of this image furnished by
NASA

Saturn is the second largest planet in the solar system, second only to Jupiter. It is nine times larger than Earth. The diameter of the planet—the measurement from one side of the planet to the other going through the center—is more than 74,900 miles.

It may be large, but it is
surprisingly light. Most
astronomers believe that Saturn
is so light that it
would float if it were
placed in an enormous
pool of water. In the
solar system, Saturn is
the sixth planet from
the Sun. It is roughly
890 million miles from
the Sun. Only Uranus
and Neptune are farther
out.

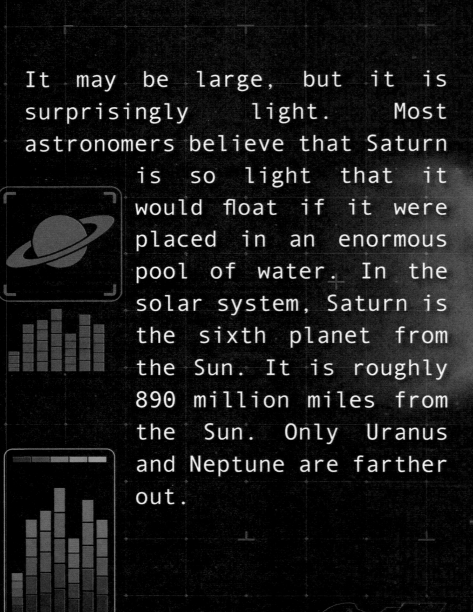

VENUS

MERCURY

EARTH

MARS

JUPITER

SATURN

URANUS

NEPTUNE

PLUTO

Solar System

All planets have two different types of movement—spin and orbit. Spin refers to how the planet pivots on its axis. Orbit is the path that the planet takes around the sun. Compared to Earth, Saturn has a fairly quick spin. It completes one rotation in less than 11 hours. That means one day on Saturn is less than half as long as one day on Earth. However, the orbit of Saturn around the Sun takes much longer than Earth's orbit.

Saturn Oppositions: 2001 - 2029

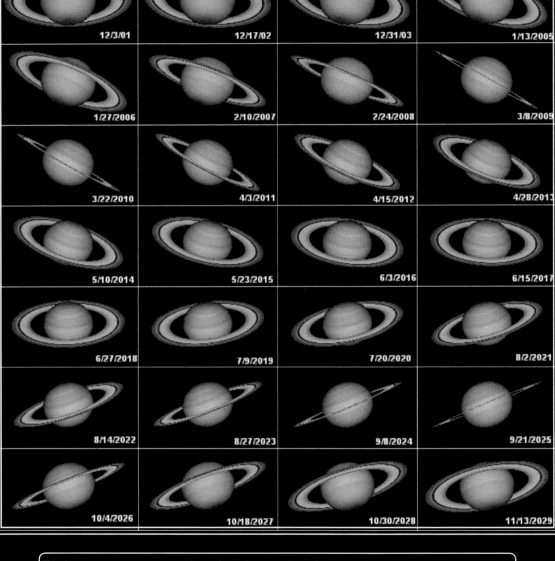

This sequence of simulated views demonstrates the
29.5-year orbital period of Saturn by opposition
date, as well as the dramatic changes in the
orientation of the planet's ring disk.

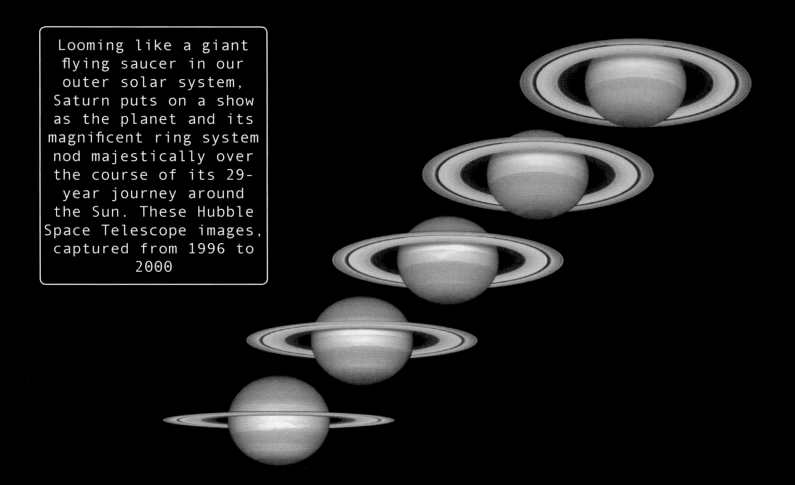

Looming like a giant flying saucer in our outer solar system, Saturn puts on a show as the planet and its magnificent ring system nod majestically over the course of its 29-year journey around the Sun. These Hubble Space Telescope images, captured from 1996 to 2000

Part of the reason for this is that Saturn is so far away from the Sun that it has a much larger path to travel. It takes the equivalent of 10,759 days for Saturn to make one trip around the Sun, while it takes the Earth about 365 days. Therefore, one year on Saturn lasts about 29 Earth years.

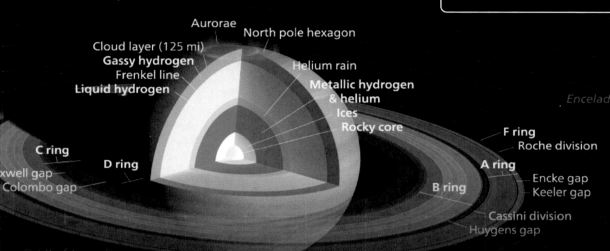

Rhea

Dione

Mimas

Aurorae North pole hexagon
Cloud layer (125 mi)
Gassy hydrogen
Frenkel line
Liquid hydrogen
Helium rain
Metallic hydrogen
& helium
Ices
Rocky core

Enceladus

Tethys

F ring
Roche division
A ring
B ring
Encke gap
Keeler gap
Cassini division
Huygens gap

C ring
Maxwell gap
Colombo gap
D ring

Orbit of Janus &
Epimetheus

There are several different kinds of planets. Saturn is known as a gas giant, meaning it lacks a solid surface and, instead, is comprised mainly of hydrogen and helium gas. Astronomers believe, however, that Saturn does have a solid core, probably a super-heated rocky center. Because Saturn spins on its axis so quickly, the gassy outer layers shift, giving the planet an odd shape.

Jupiter is an oblate spheriod

The two poles of the planet are somewhat flattened and the gas bulges at its center. This shape is called an 'oblate spheroid."

Even though Saturn is the second largest planet in the Milky Way, its gassy make-up means that it is light. In fact, Saturn is the only planet in the solar system that has a density that is less than water…about 30% less dense than water.

Planet Saturn in deep space

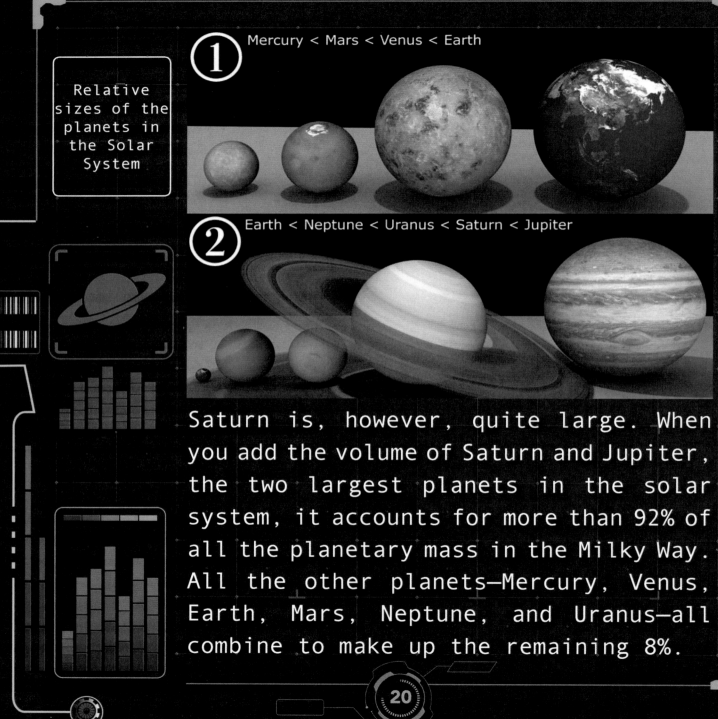

Relative sizes of the planets in the Solar System

① Mercury < Mars < Venus < Earth

② Earth < Neptune < Uranus < Saturn < Jupiter

Saturn is, however, quite large. When you add the volume of Saturn and Jupiter, the two largest planets in the solar system, it accounts for more than 92% of all the planetary mass in the Milky Way. All the other planets—Mercury, Venus, Earth, Mars, Neptune, and Uranus—all combine to make up the remaining 8%.

Saturn can be seen with the naked eye, meaning you don't need a telescope to see it. The planet has been observed for thousands of years and is noted in the folklore and mythology of many cultures around the globe. Even ancient academics and astronomers took notice of Saturn.

GEMINI

Castor

Pollux

MOON
FEB 10

Beehive Cluster

SATURN

FEB 11

FEB 12

Regulus

LEO

the view facing east a few hours after sunset will feature the moon, the Beehive Cluster, and Saturn.

For example, Babylonian astronomers kept careful record of the movements of Saturn. The ancient Greeks referred to it as a star, the ancient Romans associated it with their god of agriculture, and ancient Japanese and Chinese observers called it the 'earth star.' Early astronomers left behind plenty of writings to show us that they were aware of Saturn and its movements in the sky, but it took the invention of the telescope to discover the wonders of Saturn.

parate division parallel, including the ring.   Figure 15 rep-
ring.   Figure 16, in the latter part of the book, represents
zontal form.

would be like it, with the exception of the ring, with this
middle division.   The peculiarities of the asteroids as com-
ering that they have no rotation on their axis, then it would
that formed them.   But if it should be proven that they
ation caused by a violent rotation of the primitive planet
e a rotation on their axis, and that others actually do not,

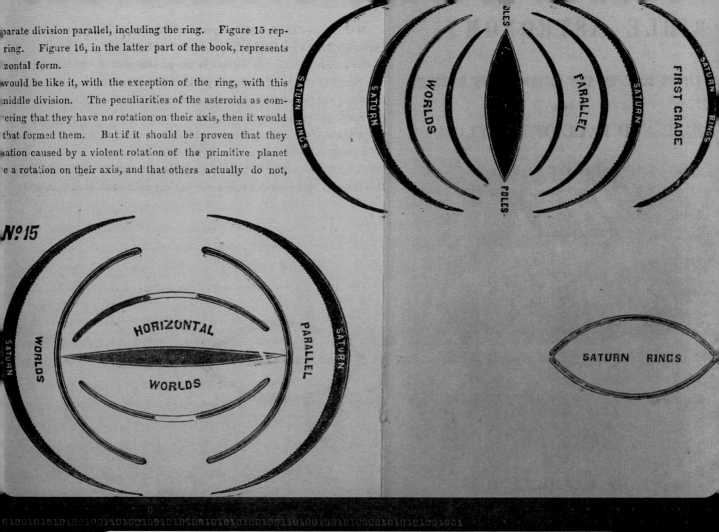

Galileo was the first person to see Saturn's rings, but with his weak telescope, he did not have a clear look at the planet. He could see two bulges on either side of Saturn, but he didn't know what he was looking at. He incorrectly assumed that he was seeing two moons on opposite sides of the planet.

Galileo Galilei

Christiaan Huygens

Forty-five years later, new technological advances led to better telescopes with more magnification ability. This was when Christiaan Huygens noted what he described as a disk encircling Saturn.

Later, in 1675, Giovanni Cassini was able to use an even more powerful telescope at the Paris Observatory to see that the disk, or ring, was not solid. He concluded that the rings of Saturn were made up of swirling space dust and debris that was orbiting the planet in a uniform way. He even noted a gap, or break, in the rings, which is now known as the Cassini Division.

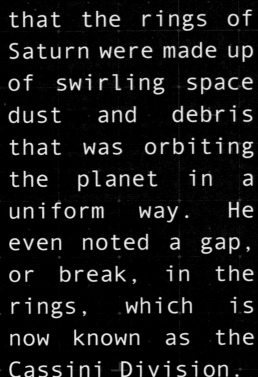

Giovanni Cassini

A Paris chez le S.r de Fer dans l'Isle du Palais sur le Quay de l'orloge a la Sphere Royale avec privilege du Roy 1705

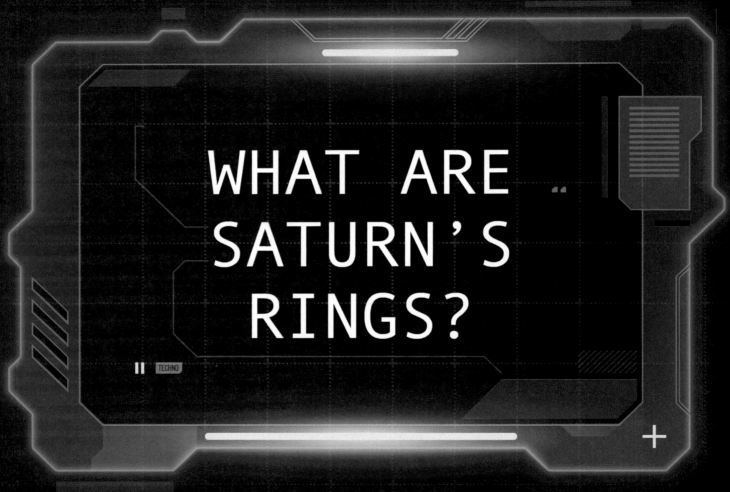

Colorful shot that shows
part of Saturn and its rings
illuminated sunbeams.

In all, Saturn is circled by a series of
seven rings. The rings form a flat, disk-
like band at the planet's equator.

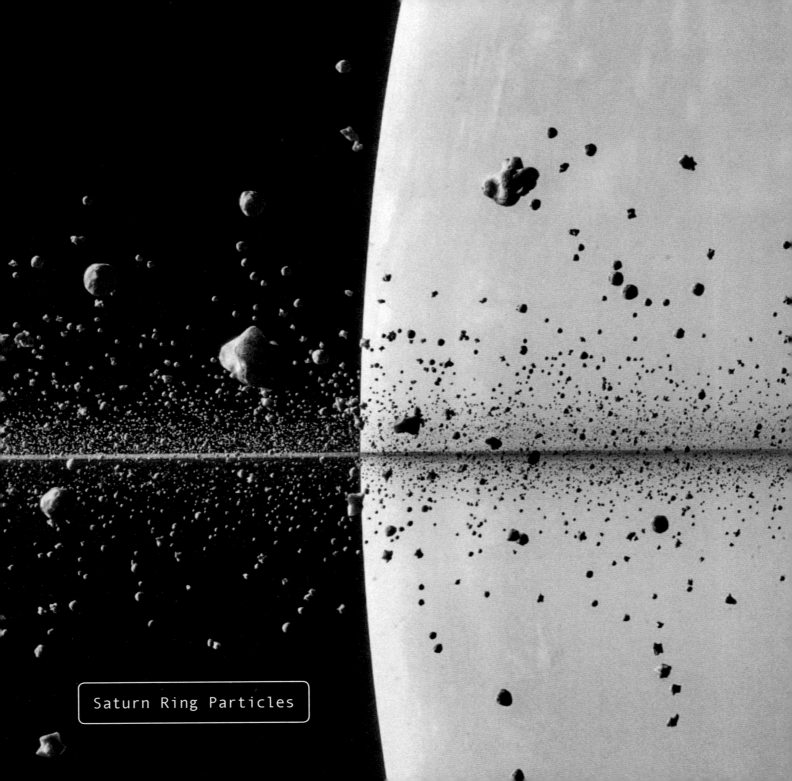

Saturn Ring Particles

Billions and billions of tiny particles made of ice and rock make up the rings. Each one would hardly be visible, but as a group, they appear almost solid.

The seven rings have been labeled by astronomers with a letter, A through G. The gaps in between them have been named for the scientists who discovered them. For example, in addition to the Cassini Division, there is the Huygens Gap.

Huygens Gap

THE MOONS OF SATURN

Planet Earth has only one moon, but Saturn has many. There are eight major moons orbiting Saturn and as many as 53 smaller ones. Saturn's moons are diverse in their make-up. Some of the moons are small chunks of rock that are classified as moonlets, or mini moons. Others are large and planet-like. Some of the moons have established orbits around the planet, while some have irregular orbits. The majority of the moons of Saturn have been named, include the larger ones, Rhea, Dione, Minas, Tethys, Iapetus, Enceladus, and Titan.

Planet Saturn and
its moons

MAJOR MOONS OF SATURN

Calypso · Methone · Mimas · Pandora · Hyperion · Rhea · Iapetus · Titan · Enceladus · Janus · Epimetheus · Prometheus · Helene · Dione · Tethys

Moons of Saturn

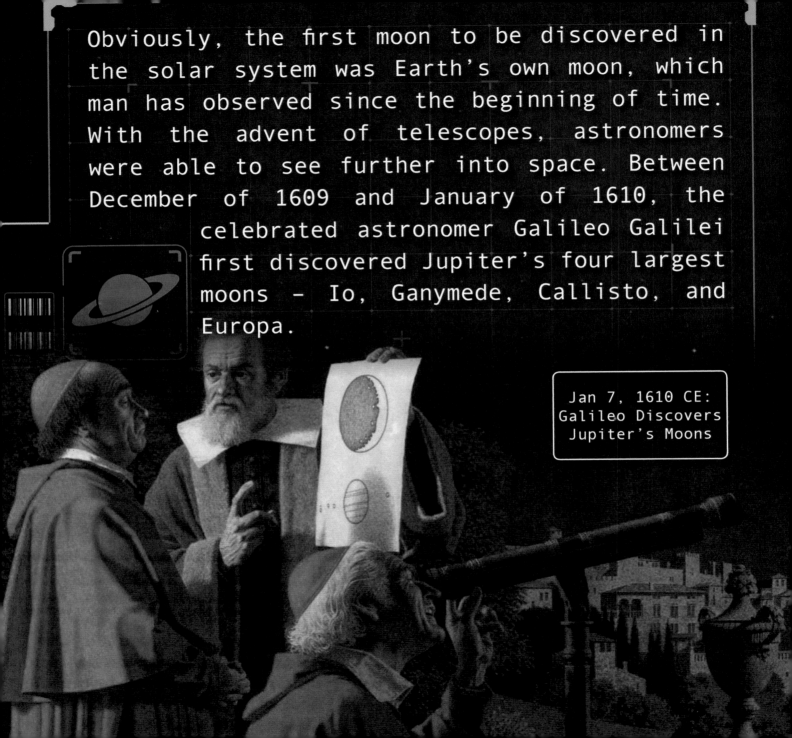

Obviously, the first moon to be discovered in the solar system was Earth's own moon, which man has observed since the beginning of time. With the advent of telescopes, astronomers were able to see further into space. Between December of 1609 and January of 1610, the celebrated astronomer Galileo Galilei first discovered Jupiter's four largest moons – Io, Ganymede, Callisto, and Europa.

Jan 7, 1610 CE:
Galileo Discovers
Jupiter's Moons

Io | Europa | Ganymede | Callisto

Collectively, these are known as the Galilean Moons. Titan was the next moon to be discovered. This happened in 1655 when the Dutch scientist, Christiaan Huygens used a more powerful telescope to peer at Saturn, its rings, and its moons.

e of Saturn's moon, Titan, is very large. In fact,
is the second largest moon in the Milky Way solar
stem. Only Jupiter's moon, Ganymede, is bigger.

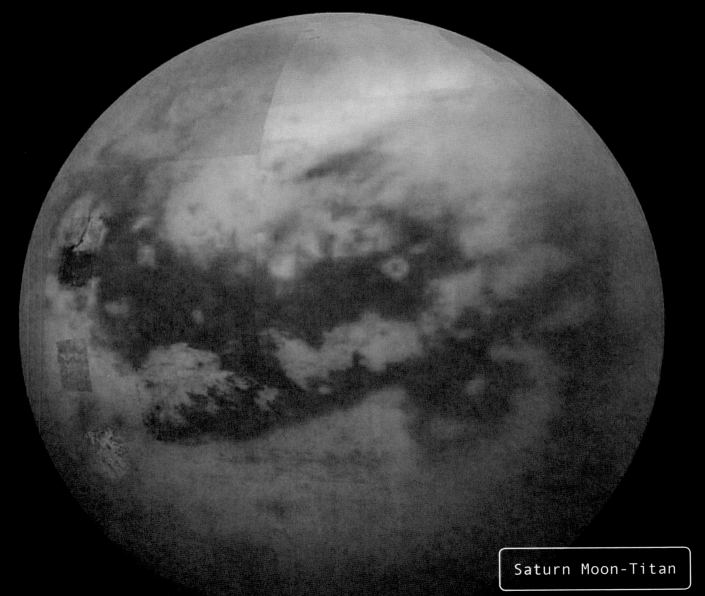

Saturn Moon-Titan

Saturn Moon Size Comparison

Mars
6,796 km
4,214 mi

Earth
12,760 km
7,926 mi

Titan
5,150 km
3,193 mi

Mercury
4,878 km
3,024 mi

Earth's Moon
3,476 km
2,155 mi

Pluto
2,274 km
1,413 mi

Titan is much bigger than the planet Mercury and twice as big as Earth's moon. Astronomers refer to Titan as a planet-like moon. Comprised of rock and ice, it is solid, unlike Saturn, and has a dense atmosphere.

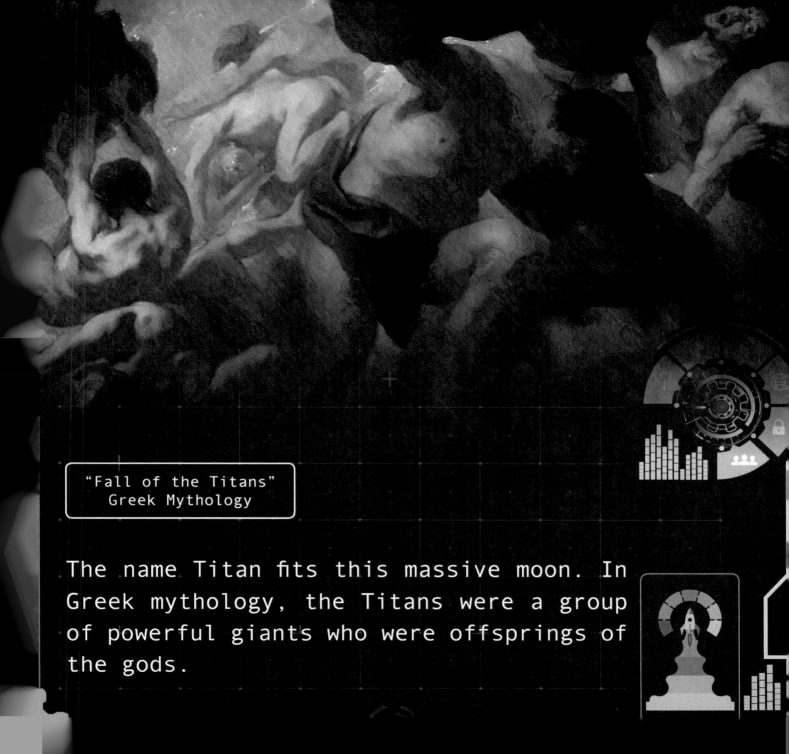

"Fall of the Titans"
Greek Mythology

The name Titan fits this massive moon. In
Greek mythology, the Titans were a group
of powerful giants who were offsprings of
the gods.

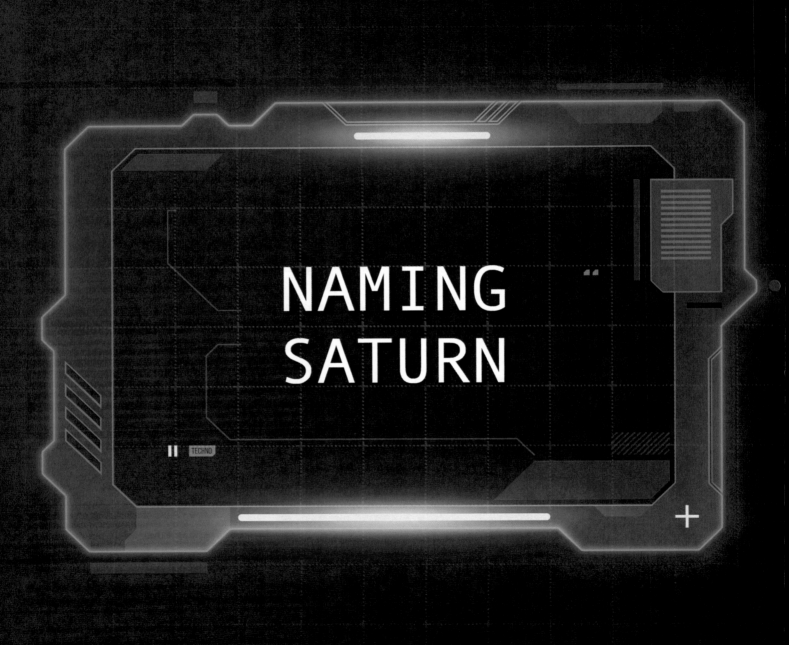

Saturn was named after the Roman god of agriculture. In fact, it was this same Roman god who lent his name to the day of the week, Saturday. The people of ancient Rome prayed to the god of agriculture to give them a bountiful harvest. A poor harvest meant disaster for ancient people who had no other food sources except for what they could grow or hunt. What began as small offerings to Saturn grew into festivals and feasts to honor this deity.

In ancient Roman religion and myth, Saturn was a god of agriculture

One such festival, Saturnalia, became the biggest and most important festival on the Roman calendar and was held every year in late December. When scientists realized the need to have just one name for each of the planets, they decided to name them after gods from Roman mythology. Saturn's moons, however, are named for figures from Greek mythology.

During his observations of Saturn, Huygens also discovered the planet's largest moon, Titan. Later, another astronomer, Jean-Dominique Cassini, realized that there are four more moons circling Saturn along with Titan and the rings. He named these moons, Rhea, Tethys, Iapetus, and Dione. All of the moons of Saturn are named for characters of Greek mythology, just like the moons of Jupiter were.

Featuring moons Iapetus, Enceladus, Dione, Tethys, Mimas, Titan, and Rhea.

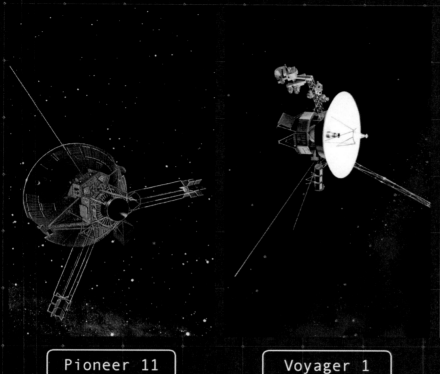

| Pioneer 11 | Voyager 1 | Voyager 2 |

Modern astronomers are just as curious about Saturn and its beautiful rings as early scientists were. In the 1970s, three different unmanned spacecraft were launched into space by the United States. Although these three crafts – Pioneer II, Voyager I, and Voyager II – were not intended to land on Saturn, they flew past the planet.

They made scientific observations and took close-up photographs of the planet. In October of 1997, NASA, the National Aeronautics and Space Administration, launched a special spacecraft called the Cassini, after the astronomer, to exclusively study Saturn. It took several years for the spacecraft to travel the distance to Saturn, and it arrived on the gas giant in June of 2004.

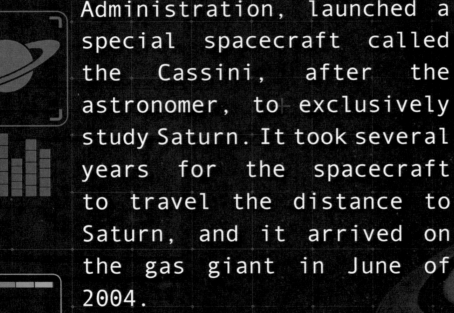

A rendering of Cassini
over Saturn and its moon
Enceladus

While the Cassini orbited Saturn, it sent down a smaller, European-made spacecraft called the Huygens, also after an astronomer, to land on the surface of Titan. On September 15, 2017, the Cassini's mission was completed, and NASA sent the spacecraft plummeting through Saturn's gassy atmosphere.

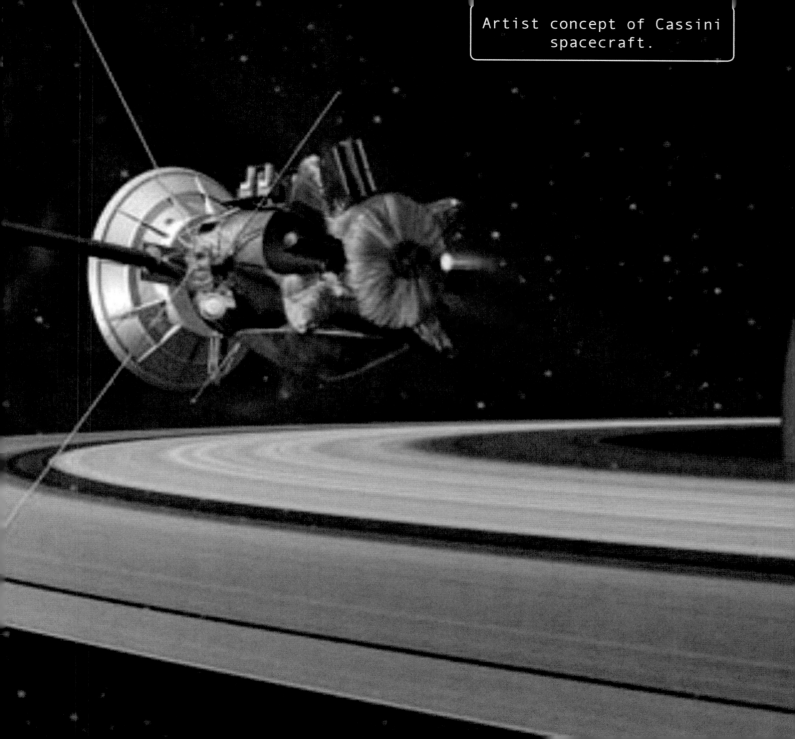

It was able to send back its last readings about the composition of the atmosphere before the spacecraft broke apart and burned up. The data that the Cassini was able to collect has been extremely valuable in our understanding of Saturn and the Milky Way solar system as a whole.

This artist's conception of the Cassini orbiter shows the Huygens probe separating to enter Titan's atmosphere.

Cassini 10 Years at Saturn
BY THE NUMBERS

2 MILLION COMMANDS executed

2 BILLION MILES TRAVELED since arrival

514 GB SCIENCE DATA collected

3039 SCIENCE PAPERS published

7 MOONS discovered

206 ORBITS completed

132 CLOSE FLYBYS of Saturn's moons

332,000 images taken

scientists from **26 NATIONS** participating

291 ENGINE burns

NASA Jet Propulsion Laboratory
California Institute of Technology

Cassini Celebrates 10 Years
Exploring Saturn

10 YEARS at SATURN

SUMMARY

Saturn is the flashiest planet in the solar system with its impressive rings. A giant ball of gas, Saturn is so vastly different than Earth that it has drawn the attention of astronomers for thousands of years. Through the use of powerful telescopes and, most recently, the Cassini spacecraft, our understanding of Saturn has increased.

Although Saturn is the most recognizable planet, each one of the eight planets in the Milky Way offer their own unique and amazing information. Now that you know more about Saturn, you should read up on the other planets to see what makes each one of them special.

Planet Saturn

Saturn's moon Enceladus and spacecraft
Cassini-Huygens in front of planet
Saturn, rings and other moons

3D rendering of Enceladus, a moon of Saturn

The Planet Saturn with
its moonsshot from space
showing all they beauty

Visit

www.BabyProfessorBooks.com

to download Free Baby Professor eBooks
and view our catalog of new and exciting
Children's Books

Made in the USA
Coppell, TX
31 January 2022

72717025R00045